The Coffee Snob

A Brief Introduction
to the Café Menu

Acknowledgements

I am grateful to the many people who have inspired me throughout the years to write this book. The list of people is endless. I suppose the greatest influence over the years has been the many shared stories with fellow baristas: Jon Foster, Deborah Bimson, Sara Hamilton, Dillon Wall, Liz Meagor, Janna Freeman and Son and Michelle Chong. The reflections and anecdotes in this brief introduction to the café menu would not be possible without the shared stories of a well cherished barista family.

If it were not for the encouragement and criticism of family and friends, this book would never have reached your hands. Enjoy.

David L. Foster

Coffee Bean Image made possible by Jeff Kubina through Wikimedia Commons, the free media repository.

Table of Contents

Preface

A "coffee snob." This is precisely what becomes of those who venture into learning the trade of the barista. Not because of any preordained expectation or any desire of the sort. It just simply happens to many of us. I say "us," because like many that have gone before me, I was once a mere consumer of this caffeinated beverage. What may be referred to as coffee snobbery didn't concern me in the least; I lacked the desire to care about something so insignificant to my day-to-day life.

That pretentious tone laced with condescension of the everyday coffee snob only finds the majority of Americans annoyed that someone would care so deeply about the quality of their coffee. What is quality coffee anyway? Where does this snobbery come from? Lastly, how is it that an education in the barista trade naturally develops such a cause to protest?

Introduction

In 2012, the number of coffee drinkers in America was an estimated 183 million, with annual trends revealing a continued growth in years to come[1]. As coffee consumption continues to rise in America, the demand for specialty café beverages (lattes, cappuccinos, macchiatos, americanos and mochas) appears to be ever increasing. Amusingly enough, it may not be a stretch to conclude that the act of consuming these café beverages has somehow aligned itself with the American dream. It seems that success for the daily 9-5 work force may in fact require that morning pick-me-up. Well, at least for the "American Dreamer."

Nevertheless, as many new-fangled coffee connoisseurs discover the hustle and bustle of the morning rush in their local coffee shop, the café menu may often leave them utterly perplexed. "What in the world is an *americano*?" they might think. This is definitely not an uncommon occurrence. With the entirety of the café menu consisting of Italian words - with the

---

[1] SBDCNet. "Coffee Shop 2012 Research Reports"

exclusion of the French beverage, the "*café au lait*" - I suppose this is quite understandable. As a barista, I can't tell you how many times I have encountered the confused stare of a customer simply trying to decode the menu that lies before them. In having been a consumer myself, prior to any barista experience, I find it easy to empathize with these customers. Thus came forth the inspiration to extend one barista's knowledge to the everyday American.

If you are a daily coffee connoisseur, newly found consumer or, perhaps merely have an interest in understanding the café menu, this is the book for you! My intent is to deliver an easy to read, an engagingly comical and very brief description of the everyday menu that you may encounter in your local coffee house.

*

While the café menu may find its origins in Italy, coffee connoisseurship throughout the world continues to change and often varies significantly from country to country. Suitably, the story of the café menu in America provides us with a perfect illustration of this.

For many of my readers, it may be a disappointment to find that there are indeed other coffee shops apart from corporate

America's famed green mermaid. For those, I am sorry to unsettle you. Before I continue, it may be appropriate to note that this book does not intend to tear down or to detest corporate coffee. Nevertheless, it would be misleading to dismiss her great influence on the everyday American coffee consumer.

Now, as we embark on our discovery of the café menu it is my hope to provide an adequate understanding of everyday café jargon, through the entertainingly comedic lens of the coffee snob. You may find that the coffee snob's pretentious gripes are an amusing tool in discovering the tradition of many café beverages.

The Latte

With no close competitor, the café latte is easily considered the most popular espresso drink in America. This American delicacy is ordered in a myriad of fashions, thanks to the explosion of sweetened syrup flavors over the years. What!? An American delicacy? Many may be surprised to learn that the café latte is not found on the menu of Italy's traditional espresso bars. It is indeed an American development. I refer to this specific espresso drink as the "American delicacy," because adult consumers in America have seemingly clung to this café beverage. Let me reiterate, "adult consumers." It is more than necessary to emphasize "adult consumers," because variations of the café latte are widely considered a child's drink to the rest of the world. Seriously?! Who would allow their child to drink coffee? Well, a significant portion of the world finds it culturally acceptable, with the obvious exception of America.

*

Café Latte Recipe:

- Espresso

- Steamed milk, with a thin layer of foam to top it off

To give a better understanding of how the majority of the coffee drinking world perceives the American connoisseurship of coffee, perhaps an illustration might be of help: While the genuine coffee snob has moved on to drinking their double espresso or café macchiato, we, the Americans, are still sucking on the 12 oz bottle of warmed milk we have grown oh-so attached to.

I do not intend to advocate openly for the American to move on to bigger and better things, beyond their morning café latte. If this is truly morning bliss, far be it from me to convince anyone otherwise. However, to the many latte drinkers who boast on their coffee snobbery, I must admit that they are gravely misinformed. And to those, please spare us the trouble and stop proclaiming that of which you know nothing, besides that watered-down (or shall I say, milked-down) flavored espresso.

In Brazil, if a boy who has never played a game before wants to play with the others, they invite him to play with the inclusion of a new set of rules, referred to as "café com leite." In declaring this set of rules, they suggest "going easy on him." Perhaps better stated, they won't hold him accountable to all of the rules; he is a beginner just learning how to play.

Quite the hilarious reference these children use in their street slang, is it not? Possibly if we are not yet convinced of our ignorance, we can now toss in the towel and plead our lack of knowledge. As much as we may hate to admit it, yes, as latte connoisseurs, we are definitely not coffee buffs – we are going easy on ourselves. So let's stop prancing around proclaiming the great taste of our coffee, when it is merely milked-down flavored espresso.

*

Nonfat Sugar-Free Vanilla Latte

Other than the traditional café latte, the nonfat sugar-free vanilla latte might be the crowd favorite. Well, at least for middle-aged folk. Often times the pressures of keeping that youthful figure get the best of us. But seriously, let's be honest. If we truly desire to make healthier choices, is the nonfat sugar-free vanilla latte really the answer? This is like a child asking for ice cream made with milk rather than cream, and sweetened with artificial sweetener rather than real sugar. Not only is this still not a healthy choice, but we have deprived the ice cream of its creamy deliciousness. Regrettably, this is the sad reality of the nonfat sugar-free vanilla latte. Let's not deprive our taste buds. If we are going to splurge, well, by all means, splurge! But let's not kid ourselves that we are making healthy life choices.

However, I can't solely blame the nonfat sugar-free vanilla latte drinker when it is not entirely their fault. It seems that the green mermaid may quite possibly be the instigator. Why, you may ask? Well, let's start by unpacking her deceptive language. If we were to visit the green mermaid, we would not place our order with the barista by saying, "a nonfat sugar-free vanilla latte, please." Rather, here is what is expected: "a skinny vanilla latte, please." Wow. Who gave her the right to change the English language? I guess she isn't breaking any laws. But seriously! Are we too careless to take notice of what she is doing? She knows exactly what the average middle-aged adult strives for. They want to feel thin, or "skinny."

The green mermaid has shrewdly won over middle-aged Americans with this café beverage by retraining them with a cleverly strung set of words. Yes, the mind is indeed being deceived. Naively, we become the sucker. Although if we are truthful with ourselves, we are okay with it. Why? Because we still get the opportunity to indulge in that sweetened and milked-down cup of coffee that we as Americans have grown quite fond of, minus the guilt. I guess we can't be too upset with the green mermaid because she has ingeniously found a way for both parties to win. She gets her revenue and we, the connoisseurs, get the drink our taste buds beg for.

Café au Lait

The café au lait could be considered the French version of the café latte. However, instead of the Italian's beloved espresso, the French concoction consists of equal parts coffee and steamed milk. Unlike the café latte, the café au lait does not traditionally come served with a steady layer of foam on top, so don't expect that beautifully fashioned, finishing touch of foam to top off this particular beverage. Nevertheless, for the American, the café au lait may be better considered a pitiable substitute for the café latte.

Is there a lesson for the connoisseur here? Yes. As a consumer, let's not scam ourselves into thinking we are trying something new when it is merely a matter of two different languages varying in moderately different tastes, with the café au lait carrying a tad stronger coffee taste. In this particular case it may be a disappointment to "branch out and try something new," so let's spare our taste buds the disappointment, and stick with those café lattes. I mean, who would really want to taste more coffee in their morning pick-me-up, when that 12 ounce cup of sweetly steamed milk is perfectly gratifying?

Surprisingly enough, if we were again to visit the green mermaid, we would not order this café beverage as the café au lait, but rather a café misto. Why the use of the Italian language to replace the better known French name? I am not entirely sure, because the café misto could hardly be considered a traditional Italian beverage. Nevertheless, the green mermaid seems perpetually to enjoy the use of an exclusive language for her customers. If only she considered the effect of these inconsistencies with other coffee houses. Or, perhaps she has?

*

In concluding my rant about the café latte, I again must propose that it is not the café latte itself that is the problem. Yes, to the greater part of the coffee world versions of it may be considered but a child's drink. Nevertheless, many Americans still find themselves craving nothing but that perfectly sweetened and milked-down cup of coffee. I am not here to judge them for that. However, again, let's not consider ourselves coffee connoisseurs or snobs while, to the majority of the coffee drinking world, we are merely overgrown children that never outgrew that sweet bottle of steamed milk. This is merely the truth of the café latte. More importantly, now we know that the café latte is purely an introductory drink to the delicately acquired taste of espresso.

The Cappuccino

After working in coffee shops for the past few years, I have discovered that the cappuccino may easily be the drink of choice for uneducated suckers, which only spoils their hope trying something new. Don't get me wrong. Traditionally, the cappuccino is held in high esteem for the everyday coffee drinker. Ironically, the cappuccino is also a cherished delight of the everyday pretentious coffee snob. An interesting contrast between consumers we might say.

To be quite frank, as Americans we have bought in to the consumerist mentality that more is better. If someone enjoys a 16 oz iced mocha, a 31 oz iced mocha must be better! And so, the green mermaid rides in on a horse, as a knight in shining armor and provides the opportunity to supersize that drink we love all too well. She is a genius. Does she care about the quality of the coffee? I'd say that's debatable. Perhaps she only concerns herself with quality if it may compromise sales, which, fortunately for her, takes no precedent in the attitude of the everyday coffee consumer in

America. Again, in her case, the green mermaid has already won over the coffee world in America, at least for the time being. I suppose I may use the phrase "coffee world" all too loosely. Once more, I propose that it is not the quality of coffee that the majority of Americans concern themselves with; rather, it is the quantity of product.

*

Cappuccino Recipe: 5-7 oz cup
- 1/3 Espresso (Double Espresso)
- 1/3 Milk
- 1/3 Foam

Now, concerning the barista's beloved cappuccino. Considering the fact that Americans have capitulated to the notion that more is better, the cappuccino becomes the ugly duckling or, perhaps better stated, the runt of the litter. The traditional cappuccino recipe consists of equal thirds of espresso, steamed milk and foamed milk prepared in a 5-7 ounce cup. What? Five to seven ounces of delight! Why on earth would anyone consider such a small portion? That is absurd. If it is such delight, would it not be more delectable in a 20 oz cup? Well then my friend, do not order a cappuccino. Order a latte, or perhaps a latte with extra foam. I say this so that the next time someone walks into their local coffee shop they are aware that ordering a 16 oz cappuccino will get them some odd looks. However, it is quite possible that the green mermaid has convinced many coffee connoisseurs that cappuccinos can be supersized if so desired, an exasperating predicament for the American barista. Traditionally, the act of supersizing such a delicacy would take away from this café beverage's genuine identity.

*

The Ignorant Cappuccino Buyer

It was another day at the coffee shop. In the morning every coffee shop is a mad house - lines running out the door, a cacophony of steam wands, espresso pulling, and blenders screaming. Impatient customers desperate for their morning fix. And so, the ordering begins...

"Good Morning Miss. How can I help you?"
"Yes, I would like a medium cappuccino to-go, please."

As the barista proceeds to grab that 8 ounce "to go" cup for the customer, while writing "Cap x2" on the cup, he is greeted by an awkward glare of confusion. Now, the barista has one of two options. Option A: Ignore the ignorant glare and proceed to place the 8 ounce cup on the bar, so the barista can continue preparing the drink, while disregarding the customer's concerns. This is perhaps the easiest way to disregard the ignorance of the consumer without having any confrontation. However, in following this course of action the barista may very well perpetuate this glare of confusion for future baristas. If so, perhaps another strategy might be a better choice. Option B: Barista responds, "Would you like your cappuccino in a larger cup, so you have more milk?" More often than not, this response will be greeted with a smile and a quick "yes, please." However, unfortunately, the cappuccino is no longer a cappuccino, it is in fact a latte with a bit of extra foam. The customer is satisfied with the sentiment of more milk, yet they are again left uneducated. This is the barista's great dilemma.

As can be seen, both options are wrong in some way or another. Option A does not provide the customer service it takes to maintain the customer's satisfaction, while *Option B* leaves the customer an uneducated coffee drinker who will only aggravate future baristas. As an experienced barista, I have witnessed this "glare of confusion" all too many times. So often in fact, that I now anticipate the expression. It almost becomes a game to the barista. If you hear the hint of a European accent, you know this person is no fool; they know their coffee well and expect that 5-7 ounce cup of pure delight. On the other hand, there may be an elderly gentleman who stares blankly at the menu for a short period with a perplexed furrowed brow before ordering a cappuccino, I'm sure by now we know what reaction is coming. Yes, the "glare of confusion" as his eyes immediately lock on that 8 ounce to-go cup. I know it seems wrong to generalize people, but trust me, 99.9% of the time these generalizations are oh so right.

*

I must say, the most aggravating part of the lack of awareness behind the cappuccino is the often found haughtiness of the customer. These stares of confusion, rooted in pride, imply to the barista that they must have indeed mistaken their order, an unfortunate reality for the barista. On the other hand, what a great opportunity it is for the barista to learn humility and restraint. If only the customer could be made aware of the exceptional service they were being given, despite their condescending ignorance. The great lengths a barista must go to to extend quality customer service often times compromise the truth of the matter. But yes, "the customer is always right."

On this note, as the barista, though you may be correct in your knowledge, you are in fact wrong because the customer's satisfaction is more important than your genius. Yes, it's unfortunate, I know. Regrettably, even worse, the green mermaid has won by selling this grand slogan, "the customer is always right." Why is this? Well, as humans we hate to be wrong of course! So why not sell their customers the falsified reality that they are always right, even when they have been gravely mistaken. People love this! Who wouldn't want to buy into this notion? I'd be more than happy with people accepting my knowledge without having to give reason for it. Life would seem a bit easier I suppose. Again, the green mermaid is brilliant in her craftily developed marketing techniques. It's not the quality of coffee people are buying, it is their dignity.

Imagine if we, as humans, used this model to raise our children. If a child first refered to all four-legged animals by muttering the words "kitty-cat," we would simply accept the notion as true, because we would not want to insult the child's lack of knowledge with the truth. This is an outlandish notion, right? We would never consider such a model of child rearing. So why is it that we choose to buy into this model for ourselves in adulthood? It seems that as adults we have grown too old and have acquired too much "wisdom" ever to be wrong. And so to the everyday American the cappuccino will be, at least for the time being, deprived of its genuine identity and complete and utter delightfulness. One could hope that its true identity will soon be resurrected, so the barista no longer has to play the fool.

The Macchiato

If the cappuccino is the preferred drink of the "broaden your horizon" type of sucker in the American coffee world, the café macchiato could easily be considered the drink for the misinformed. To the overwhelming majority of coffee drinkers in America, the term "macchiato" finds its identity in the widely popularized and sweetly pleasurable drink known to America as the "caramel macchiato." Oh, that perfectly crafted masterpiece of sweetened heavenly delight and its uniquely configured caramel drizzle floating atop that flawlessly poured cloud of foam. By now, many of my readers may be caught drooling over the thought of such a sugary goodness. However, unfortunately, for those that have been caught drooling, this is not the macchiato known to the rest of coffee world.

*

Café Macchiato Recipe:

- Espresso
- Lightly topped off with a dollop of foam, sometimes with a touch more of steamed milk (depending upon one's preference)

*

As you may have noticed from the recipe above, the café macchiato resembles nothing of the popularized drink known to America as the "caramel macchiato." To make matters worse, many of America's daily "caramel macchiato" consumers have begun to shorten their language use, now simply referring to this caramel delight as a "macchiato" - a travesty for the barista. Again, we find that the language known to the traditional coffee world has been tampered with. By now, I'm sure it may not be a stretch to find where this discrepancy originated. Yes, look no further than America's adored green mermaid. The caramel macchiato is indubitably the innovation of America's favorite coffee venue. But wait, the green mermaid has not only altered the English language to sell their product, but she may also be found guilty of redefining words in the Italian language.

I suppose "redefining" might be taking it a bit far. In Italian the term *macchiato* literally means "marked" or "stained." So in the case of the café macchiato, the espresso has been stained with a dollop of foam. Coincidently, the caramel macchiato in reality just an upside down latte (meaning the shots are poured on top) - finds its definition in being marked by the caramel drizzle rather than that delicate touch of foam. Nonetheless, in coining the name of this café beverage, the green mermaid is unquestionably misleading America's coffee consumers with her linguistic inconsistencies. Italian culture holds a high standard of maintaining tradition, with commitment to quality, while ironically, our green mermaid comes along and reinvents the barista's menu. I suppose this is the story of America. American companies tend easily to stray away from the concern for quality, because

American consumers are arguably more preoccupied with the accessibility and quantity of the product.

All of this is to say, if I may profess, the undertaking of being an American barista is not always easy. As the lines are running out the door with people desperate for their morning pick-me-up, the continued lack of coffee awareness and language discrepancy proves to be a difficult task to interpret across the bar. Let me again provide a brief illustration:

"The Café Macchiato Customer"

As the sun begins to set in the evening, the intoxicating aromas of a coffee house lure in a different type of customer. On a cozy Wednesday evening, is there not a more suitable destination to take that pretty gal out for the first time? Well, in one young gentleman's case, the coffee shop is the place to be. I suppose a coffee house environment gives off that soothingly mellow vibe that is certainly conversation friendly. In his mind, everything has been thought out perfectly just as the evening is about to commence. But wait, as the man approaches the bar he realizes he has no idea as to what to order. He proceeds to approach the bar with confidence, while briefly glancing over the menu. Suddenly, a familiar term catches his eye, and with great assurance he orders, "a macchiato, please."

More often than not, as the barista you know that this probably is not the drink that the customer would prefer to complement his evening with. However, as the young gentleman ordered with such confidence, the barista is hardly phased and subsequently shoots the order over to the espresso bar. It may be presumed that this young man was seeking to give the illusion that he knew what he was ordering, so his date might notice his assertiveness as a male. Needless to say, his date follows up by ordering her regular drink, "may I have the white mocha with extra whipped cream."

As they walk over to the bar to wait for their drinks, the gentleman hears his drink being called by the barista, "café macchiato!" Now again, the barista on the bar is well aware that this might not be the drink the young gentleman really desired. And so, the barista pauses to observe the man as he looks at his tiny 8 oz to-go cup that is merely half filled. A perplexed look of discontentment soon fills the young man's face. The inner dialogue of the barista was indeed correct yet again. Nonetheless, filled with pity, the barista proceeds to suggest, "Sir, I have some extra steamed milk in the pitcher if you'd like it filled to the brim." This considerate gesture is promptly agreed to, as the gentleman grins and quickly replies, "Sure, that sounds great." Phew, that was a close one. Now the young man's confidence has been restored, so that he may continue on with the rest of his date.

*

Now, what happened here? The young gentleman innocently ordered a "macchiato," while under the impression that he knew what it was. Is this lack of knowledge his fault? Perhaps, in his overconfidence, he may be blamed. However, I do not suppose that this is the problem. The real problem is the term *macchiato* itself. Well, at least the wide-spread misconception of the term that has been marketed across the country via our adored friend, the green mermaid.

As the green mermaid incessantly redefines the coffee house menu with her special language, I must again propose that she is subsequently winning the American coffee world over. Why is this? As the special language becomes more and more wide-spread, due to the continuous expansion across the world, people are being trained to drink exclusively green mermaid coffee. It's like the case of Pavlov's dog. Just as Ivan Pavlov trained his dog, the green mermaid has learned to train her customers through the use of a special language. When versed green mermaid customers choose to venture out and visit their local coffee house, they are found to be ignorant in their coffee jargon. This makes us uncomfortable, and so we quickly find ourselves moseying on back to the old stomping ground to visit our pal, the green mermaid.

May I again point out her ingenious marketing techniques! At the cost of forfeiting the precision of language by rewriting a new one, the green mermaid has discovered that she can win big with American connoisseurs. What a travesty this has created for today's barista.

The Americano

For the everyday American connoisseur, the Italian's most esteemed café selection, the espresso or double espresso, is an afterthought. Why an "afterthought" you may ask? A multitude of reasons could be brought forth in defense. However, if I were to find a place to start, I must assert that America's coffee culture has become much more concerned with the extent of time an individual has to relish their café beverage, which inevitably leaves the espresso, and its twin the double espresso, out of the equation. Consequently, we have replaced the Italian's beloved espresso on the café menu with our greatly treasured americano, which may easily be considered a deplorable substitute. The American connoisseur might, in time, learn to appreciate the Italian's divinely inspired espresso and gently acquired taste, but for now it remains merely a condiment for our cup of water and steamed milk.

*

Americano Recipe:

- Espresso
- Water

*

Yes, amusingly enough, not only does America neglect to appreciate the skillfully prepared espresso and its genuine art form, but we have proceeded to deride its unique excellence with the addition of large quantities of water. Before I continue, I suppose a historical account of where the americano received its famed name is in order. According to legend, the americano was given its name during the time of World War I. During WWI, the American GIs would often visit the Italian cafés where, without question, drip coffee was not served. Unfortunately for them, the only caffeine producing machines around were those that served espresso. This has got to be some sick joke! One to two ounces of beverage is simply not enough to compliment a morning with. Nevertheless, the Americans discovered a genius remedy for this. After ordering their espresso, they decided that pouring water over it would give them that long lasting café beverage experience they desperately needed so they could to do their morning right.

Could you imagine witnessing this grand mockery? Some of my readers may question me in saying, "grand mockery." However, let me illustrate. Unlike some American baristas (I only say "some" because there are those that do care), the Italian barista takes great pride in their espresso pulling and café presentation. That being said, let's put ourselves in the Italian barista's shoes. Imagine this: an American soldier walks into an espresso bar and orders a double espresso. Shortly after, he is handed a perfectly pulled double espresso. He then takes the espresso, dumps it into a larger cup, and proceeds to pour water out of his canteen over the top of it. What!! Is this guy serious? Not only has he destroyed the crema of the espresso and stripped it of its sweet caramel inspired taste, but he has watered down perfection at its finest. The heartbreak. Okay, so maybe that is a bit of an overly dramatic illustration. Nevertheless, perhaps this illustration may help us understand why the rest of the coffee world scoffs at the American idea of coffee connoisseurship.

This, according to legend, is how the americano received its name. And yes, the name itself carries an undertone of sarcasm, which certainly implies contempt toward the American's pitiable choice in coffee. I suppose it may be appropriate to refer to this café beverage as the "American espresso."

*

The Espresso:

For some strange reason, Americans accept the terribly misconceived notion that straight espresso is dreadfully bitter, which in turn leads to the idea that much milk or water is necessary for one's enjoyment of it. What an unfortunate belief this is! Moreover, how greatly erroneous! Perhaps this false notion stems from the probability that many Americans have never had the opportunity to taste freshly prepared, quality espresso done right.

For the Italian barista, there is a precise technique used in the art of pulling quality espresso. This technique is most simply explained through the Four Italian M's:

1. *Macinazione*: The proper grind

2. *Miscela*: The quality of coffee beans

3. *Macchina*: The Espresso Machine

4. *Mano*: The hand of the barista

If each of these four "M's" were to be strictly followed, we will soon find ourselves enjoying that perfectly crafted and velvety sweet taste of freshly pulled espresso. Velvety sweet taste? Yes, I reiterate, "velvety sweet taste." I must again propose, however, that there is a significant chance that many Americans have never had the privilege of tasting this genuine art form. Sadly, Americans have never even made the attempt to try straight espresso, due to our previously stated bogus disposition. In fact, straight espresso is never even considered.

Concerning the espresso, the majority of coffee houses in America probably will meet the first three Italian "M's": the grind, the beans and the machine. However, regarding the fourth "M," the American barista's hand, I must grimly admit that many continue to try and fail, while delivering our morning pick-me-up. Yes, there is a significant chance that many everyday coffee drinkers are being served sub-par or even poor quality espresso more often than not. Some of us may find ourselves saying, "C'mon how hard can pulling a shot of espresso be?" Well, for many, not hard at all. Why should they be concerned with the quality of the espresso, when the consumer chooses to dilute its genuine taste with large amounts of milk, water and syrupy sweetener? Let's not get ahead of ourselves here, and pretend that we actually care about the quality of the espresso, when we do not intend to stray from our habitual routine of sweetened and milked-down espresso. For the American, the espresso is merely the means to an end, which is caffeine, and this is our only concern. This is precisely why we are left uneducated in the art of the espresso, while we continue to find contentment in those watered down cups.

The Mocha

What better place to conclude our journey through the café menu than with the oh so famous café mocha? For those who proclaim coffee to be too bitter for their taste, look no further! With this café beverage, let me formally welcome you to the coffee drinking world. Many consider the café mocha "the gateway drug to coffee," due to its irresistible taste and potentially addictive nature.

For some, this chocolaty delight's wooing influence may be overpowering, yet there are several who could never imagine abandoning this wonderfully pleasing concoction. Chocolate and espresso? Who could have conceived such greatness? Oh wait, we're talking about chocolate. Of course this is how people could be effortlessly won over as regular coffee consumers! Not many could turn down the opportunity to satisfy their caffeine need with a nice cup of steamed hot chocolate (not to forget the espresso).

*

The Café Mocha Recipe:
- Chocolate
- Espresso
- Steamed Milk
- Topped with a fittingly swirled layer of whipped cream

*

Yes, the café mocha is simply a latte with the addition of chocolate. Due to its overwhelming popularity, it acquired its own distinguishable name on the café menu. Just the other day, I visited a local coffee house with a friend who is not much of a coffee person, and he, in fact, placed his order with the barista asking, "Can I get a chocolate latte, please." While this is technically what he wanted, my friend was greeted with a confused stare and a slight chuckle before he was corrected with, "Did you mean a café mocha?"

With this genius creation sweetly welcoming in new coffee drinkers by the truck load, it was only a matter of time before the now beloved sweetened syrups to hit the scene in America. The unending supply of various flavors consisting of fruit, nut and spice sweetened syrups opened the door to coffee for the everyday sweet-tooth. And of course, the green mermaid has resourcefully used this flavor array to reinvent the café menu. As many Americans search for that sugar fix, the green mermaid has so kindly written us the perfect menu. By recreating the café menu knowing that Americans are ever so hesitant to stray away from sweetened beverages - she has again won over our hearts. Well, at least our taste buds.

What else would we expect? Here we are America, years down the road proclaiming to be coffee connoisseurs and snobs, or something of the sort. Yet, are we actually coffee connoisseurs who are passionate about the quality of coffee in our morning cup? I'd say that is a bit of a stretch. Or are we just caffeine addicts looking for any way to "help the medicine go down?" I suppose this is quite possibly the case for many of us. It seems that the introduction of the café mocha, along with all of the other flavored drinks, has unfortunately prevented American connoisseurs from discovering the authentic taste of espresso.

Conclusion

Congratulations! You are now well versed in the everyday lingo found on the café menu. I hope my comically informative presentation has provided you with the knowledge to confidently endure the madness of those morning crowds.

Now, for the everyday American, it seems that coffee has been defined, perhaps even linguistically monopolized, by none other than our beloved green mermaid. Whether we know it or not, to some extent, the knowledge we may have previously acquired concerning the café menu was a result of her great influence. And so, at least for the time being, it seems that she will continue to sit on her throne, imparting her inaccurate knowledge to the American people while simultaneously striving to reach her arms out to the greater parts of the world.

Although this may be the case, it seems that coffee trends are beginning to reveal a divergence in course and preference in connoisseurship. The concern for quality over quantity has never been more evident in the American coffee drinker than it is now.

As the appreciation for the origins of the café menu are finding their way back to the American coffee house, it will be interesting to discover the tactics of these larger corporations to remain afoot. Don't get me wrong; I don't intend to project their demise. There will always be those who prefer to remain in the American coffee way, as it has been introduced in this book. Therefore, the demand will undoubtedly exist.

It may be that these two notions of coffee connoisseurship will divide markets entirely, which seems to be the case. I suppose only time will tell. Whether you embrace the American tradition of coffee or are influenced by the café menu's origin is entirely up to you. Nevertheless, I hope this newly acquired knowledge of the café menu allows you to order your café beverage of choice with great confidence.

Made in the USA
San Bernardino, CA
02 November 2014